GHOSTS

poems by

Nancy L. Davis

Finishing Line Press
Georgetown, Kentucky

GHOSTS

Copyright © 2019 by Nancy L. Davis
ISBN 978-1-63534-971-9 First Edition
All rights reserved under International and Pan-American Copyright Conventions. No part of this book may be reproduced in any manner whatsoever without written permission from the publisher, except in the case of brief quotations embodied in critical articles and reviews.

ACKNOWLEDGMENTS

"Luminesce," *Point of View*, 2014
"Firestorm: Checagou," *Philadelphia Stories*, Winner, Sandy Crimmins National Prize in Poetry; nominee for 2018 Pushcart Prize
"Ghosts," *CUTTHROAT, A Journal of the Arts*, Finalist, 2017 Joy Harjo Poetry Prize
"Sanctuary," Semi-Finalist, 2018 Pablo Neruda Poetry Competition, *Nimrod*

Publisher: Leah Maines
Editor: Christen Kincaid
Cover Art: Richard A. Cappellitti
Author Photo: Richard A. Cappellitti
Cover Design: Nancy Rosenbaum

Printed in the USA on acid-free paper.
Order online: www.finishinglinepress.com
also available on amazon.com

Author inquiries and mail orders:
Finishing Line Press
P. O. Box 1626
Georgetown, Kentucky 40324
U. S. A.

Table of Contents

Sanctuary 1

Mating 3

This Is Love 4

Still Life 5

Ghosts 6

Trajectory 7

Entrances 9

Into the Garden: Dreamscape 11

Luminesce 13

Musings 15

Desire 16

Firestorm: Checagou 20

Love's Loss 23

In June 24

History Lessons 25

for Rick and Julia

"The world is full of magic things,
patiently waiting for our senses to
grow sharper."

—W.B. Yeats

Sanctuary

the dead are buried here,
contaminated fish bones compressed into
strata of an unintended geological age;
radioactive skulls the stuff of *Dia de los Muertos*

wolves run free along fertile
riverbanks, whooping and howling
under a pink spring moon: this is their turf now,
brash physicists and engineers
long gone, unfettered fruit trees
blossoming profusely, pushing through window
casements of once-tidy brick homes,
the flowers' heavy scent a quixotic mix
of wild musk and memory.

the rare black stork nests atop light posts,
harbinger of a dangerous secret, that
a nuclear rebirth has hatched in The Zone,
the hulking Reactor a menacing reminder
of all that goes wrong.

poachers cross boundaries, at their own
risk, when ingesting a single wild hair
can set them off. Beavers, bison, bears, badgers
call this place home. Giant catfish swarm
rebounding streams—drainage canals
and wheat fields vestigial producers
of past wealth.

four-hundred times the contaminants of
Hiroshima, the aftermath haunts
organs and sinews, yet yowling
wolf packs flourish, Chevalskis*
return, white-tailed eagles
swoop and slope.

*wild horses native to the region

in the rusted shadows of civilization's greatest
nuclear disaster, the red forest stuns green,
a ferris wheel sits innocent, animal populations
burgeon, and the old Jewish trading post of
Chernobyl logs its final transaction in the ledgers
of our starkly short-lived history.

Mating

it is a copious affair,
multiple couples coupling, floating
in a fount of ecstasy, bubbles
emanating sounds
growling and guttural, rippling
in watery effervescence

what does the cold-blooded female feel
from the sandy banks of this fetid swamp?
some primordial ache, an urgency so visceral
she responds in supple strides, inviting the
ritual each season, cold heart
beating, blood coursing, lustful Cleopatra eyes
protruding like periscopes above her liquified bed
of pleasure

impossibly fluid, graceful, she demurs
only for the sake of her corporeal urge, the ancient
pulse of procreation as robust as the hundred-pound
tail slapping, sweeping unwary predators from
the carefully constructed mud-stick nest buried
deep in the primeval consciousness
of a consummate survivor

This Is Love

I tend to my dying dog like the Devout anointing the feet of a Saint. Fighting a two-year battle, she won't go easily; stubbornness floods her veins, lifted her from Chicago's cold streets straight into my arms one autumn. I am her Sun, her alpha goddess; she follows my attendant moves with milky eyes, the viscosity of which would make a newly-milled engine fail.

Once leaping off all fours some ancient part of her was bred to do, she claws her way up the oak-floor steps—unforgiving in their glossy treachery—to sleep by our side. I bring her water at each landing, a baptismal font of love and eternal life, coax her every move, wheedling with healthy treats, ever organic: we will not poison the noble path she has led from runaway, stray, mother, reluctant pet to transcendent being, reborn a fifth time to protect her family to the death.

I surprise myself. The accidents are many; doctor visits, bills unending; my back bent with prodding. I was not always so patient, the demands of living too taxing to coddle her gnawing pain, distended belly, arthritic forelegs turned inward in a kind of perverse supplication.

Who can determine at what point through this final passage we bow our heads in the humility of selflessness, as, ministering a cocoon of gauzy comfort—a winding sheet wrapped in compassion—we lift corporeal to spirit, and live the better for it?

Still Life

Part One: Water Garden

sapphire skies, strong winds
undercurrent bellying up
sail untethered—stillborn

Part Two: Isadora's Convertible

freedom at a cost
scarf unraveling loosely
wheel of fortune no more

Ghosts
> *Rawa-Ruska, Ukraine**

Mud-slick spring, and
a fallow field rises and falls in
sepia tones, forsythia blooming
in brambling chaos.

Strange this swath of land
should stretch stillborn in
the fertile season.

No cairns mark its meaning,
no stones mask its passage
from profane to sacred.

Like a mole, blind in its star-starved
pursuit of light—a tuberous longing
for air where deep dark rumblings echo
a tragic chorus, muffled
and silenced.

Far up the hillside, a mausoleum
of memory haunts. Children play
in the dirt, tunnel sluices to catch
and carry seasonal torrents.

Mummified for generations,
desiccated in grim awareness: the
grotesque grave dance a
choreography of horrors buried in
the hollow
of a village's topography.

---

*Site of a mass grave of Eastern European Jews, murdered by SS Mobile Killing Squads

Trajectory
      in memoriam: denial

it is always this way
on a Wednesday,
no matter the season:
cerulean skies, whipped winds
meringue-licked white caps
and the arc of your path
seared into memory.

did you surface-dance away that
first hour, shifting expertly
swinging attention to the muse
of your course? did you
plan your journey,
or were you on a
mission of abandon—
not the reckless kind
but a letting go, as, easing the tension
in the mast's rope,
you traversed the angles
of your life's passions:
beautiful wife, devoted son
supportive family and friends,
sterling accomplishments enough
to fill three lifetimes—
dexterous fingers
nimble mind
your focus a marvel,
never diverted

except
on
this day.

did you not notice the
boatlessness of your Great Lake,
crafts called off in warnings of

imminent and threatening
scale?

or was it too mild a morning,
too lovely
the way the breeze rippled in
wavelets and the sandy shores
like down comforters tumbling easily
into languid liquidity
called you out as, stealthily, sturdily, steadily,
you slipped into your skin of
preference, and,
breaking the waters,
traveled another lifetime—
a sailor's passage of
the unaccountable—compression and release,
your body-soul returning
days, not years later

a modern-day Odysseus
dutifully
come home.

Entrances
> *sorrow*

To say that door will never
open the same way—
the shoulders through your leather jacket
erect, strong
soft shadings of light patterning
the sleeves and reaching
squared cuffs that frame
the knowing, capable hands
of metal-surgeon-musician-photographer-
sailor soaring into underwater
tapestries of sea and lake life
hands that hold the door
ring flashing gold
with the love of your life
your wife—
her auburn hair chestnut in the light
that trails her black wool coat
tailored with etched ebony
buttons, embroidered braiding
lacing
the folds.

To say we've stepped
through the threshold
of friendship
a last time—
that must last time—
the arc of your arm
holding the door and
brushing against the
jamb the steady
creak voicing
your entrance   no need
to ring or knock   the
familiarity a gift as
sacred as your silhouette

the last time you walked
through that door
the cloth of your cloak
bracing embracing
darkness and light

Into the Garden: Dreamscape
acceptance

in the lake house on the bluff
a woman opens her door
peering out somewhere between
dusk and remembrance

we stand nearby
huddled in honeysuckle,
dusky hydrangeas eluding
our grasp, their petals
bunched in papery clamor

our voices, husky with evening,
belie the crunch of gravel
beneath our shoes that follow
a serpentine path

I am eager to show you
my new plantings:
bright dahlias and daisies, prim
foxglove, shy coral bells bordering
mounds of freshly shredded mulch:
hardwood pining for resurrection,
redemption

I want so much to take
your hand,
lead you to shelter

You always were the gardener,
you say—
startling me out of deep-blue silence,
nighthawks piercing the sky
like arrows dancing in arabesque—
I always admired your patient urging,
nudging shallow roots to dig deeply
into life, to hold on like death,
to drink greedily the loamy liquid

I nod with modesty,
search the eyes of the woman at the door
who shifts, now, uneasily
looks down, flattening wind-worn hands
against muslin skirt, dismayed to be the one
to say, *You cannot enter the house
of the living*

we watch as darkness settles in her eyes like
swallows nestling into cavernous
thoughts at sundown
I watch as you plant your feet firmly
into the soil of the
afterlife
musk-phlox and wild lilies luminescing
in lilac-and-melon moon glow

and all the while
cricket choirs brimming with psalms of
sorrow and longing
sing over and over and over the
verses and refrains echoing
resonating the loveliness the magnificence
the aching nostalgia
of nightfall

Luminesce
> *for Nonna*

In a deep-blue corner
of morning where
25th Street meets Stewart,
the hill rises like a church spire
to the neighboring heavens
above. The swing sets ready to rock;
crisp laundered sheets snap
to attention, hang
with the precision and grace
of one who knows the
value of a job well done,
the mourning dove's urging to
forget me not.

Blood-red greens of a
rhubarb leaf—
succulent and bitter—
turn toward the sun
splashing gold on the modest
acreage below:
lawn edges cropped and tidy,
vegetable plots bordered with bricks,
sidewalks parchment white.

Out the window facing east
day widens with
lavender hues of sunrise.
Dishes in the sink, yellow kettle
on the stove, the whistling
sustenance dipped in honey
rising like the slow hum
of trains passing by—
pear-tree blossoms
raining in the yard where

forget-me-nots
steal glory from May stories

(peonies flush with pretty, perfumed in Baroque),
their periwinkle blues pulling
up, breaking through, forging roots in
the inhospitable—blanched earth, caved concrete—
living on air and light and water
only the faithful know.

Love the eager blooms
in noontime illumination
transcending time, space and cultivation,
singing, *look at me*; clustered beauties too
modest to fuss. Forget not the love:
Listen as its florescence rustles
tall grasses, glows amid
moonlit branches, rises awash
each dew-dawn day
like a newborn flush
with gratitude.

Musings
> *three in the classroom*

In the back of the room sit
the three Muses:
Rudi, Loquacious and Starstruck.

Rudi spins her piano stool
searching for music caught in
melodies of
her past.

Loquacious presses against
doors, hinges rusted
with disuse;
lintels dusty and warped.

Starstruck pounds
fleshy tentacles
on ancient
barnacled rocks.

The others,
poised and brooding,
sit scattered
like so many vessels

Anchored in tradition,
and musing
whether catching the notes
in the spine of her voice,
slipping over thresholds
of splintered pasts,
or sifting through centuries
of archaeological digs

Won't be enough
to silence each in
prayer and
in awe.

Desire

I.   Interloper
She squeezed teal-blue into
forest-green to catch the varying hues borne
by the quaking light of a mid-August afternoon.
Cicadas deafened; bluebirds crisscrossed the meadow
once routinely groomed by Pirate and Stunner, her Morgan
and Bay—the stable empty now, save random barn cats
or the insistent wasp nest. She lay the paint tubes side by
side, patient allies in her struggle to perfect.

A holly branch heavy with crimson strained and snapped
at the base of the hill, the crackling sound sizzling like
oil popping in a scalding pan. She studied the velvety shadings
of the woodlands deep below, held her breath for a shock of
movement. A frightened flock of finches spun out from
a honeysuckle patch, kaleidoscopic sun streaks shooting like
luminous arrows into her view.

All at once it appeared: barreling out of its musky secrecy,
voracious demeanor, ambling with surprising speed and grace
up the hillside, clawing madly with one massive, capable paw
at the foliage caught in its thick, black pelt.

Perched high on the second-story balcony of her studio, she sat
safe in the moment. But the structure stood on stilts. The beast
could scale it in seconds, she knew full well, if it so desired. She
glanced at her canvas, searching for the vision in the painting's expert
rendering, precise angling, subtle shading—and found none.

Low grumbles, stubborn grunts ricocheted across the ravine in
staccato measures, like the throaty vibrato of warblers,
accentuating the cautious distance between herself and the Bear.
Then, a ghastly mechanical whir of the lawn mower filled the air. Her
husband had begun his chores. Now, she thought, this Sunday afternoon,
when he'd had the weekend.

Startled, the Bruin reared on hind legs, surveying its place in the
world, and—lowing a deep, guttural growl—pitched backward in a
perfect pirouette. Shoulders moving like a well-oiled machine
beneath its sable coat, its enormous body lumbered in long,
eager strides back down the slope.

Hands trembling, she placed the painting on the easel,
allowing it to dry unfinished in the diminishing sun. *Clarissa*,
she yelled, foolishly; no one could hear, yet worrying whether
their daughter had returned from her neighbor-friend's house a
quarter-mile down the road. She fumbled for her phone, instinctively,
then recalled it sat inert on the kitchen counter inside the house.
Better not to frighten with chatter, she reasoned, unconvinced.

She looked across the yard to her husband for guidance. He sat erect
on the cushioned seat of the Toro, his ears padded with soundproofed
headphones. He glanced up, likely feeling her eyes on him, and pointed
to the gully where the animal had been, motioning an enthusiastic
thumbs up. What was so good about a bear invading their home? she
wanted to know. *Bears don't know property lines*, she knew he'd retort.
Their land, too. So casual, so terse, she thought. All knowing:
some Adonis she'd taken it into her heart to marry twelve years before,
desire canceling out all else. We'll see, she cursed under her breath.
We shall see.

II.   Procrastination
As early as spring, bear stories circled the valley
like hungry hawks. It unsettled her, he knew. Much as she
loved their ten acres, she wasn't one for the wild. Take the coyote
pack yipping and yawing over its rabbit catch right outside their
window under moonlight their first night here. The prey screaming
like a newborn and waking his wife out of a pregnancy dream.

Maybe it was his training—an Eagle Scout at eighteen. Two-week
survival canoe trips in the dense wilderness of the Adirondacks, ten
suburban boys to account for, no less, their own whining a constant
reminder that some humans simply are too far removed from the

natural world to recognize their place in it.

Or maybe it was the thrill to think these predators still thrived: a bobcat padding stealthily in the morning dew early autumn as he drove Clarissa to pre-school one day. His own penchant to test himself in the extreme: winter camping expeditions with male soul mates— the deeper below zero, the better. What was the measure of a man, after all, he reasoned: the crisp corners of a stack of bills or how quickly he could fan a fire on a frigid February morning, four-foot snow drifts buffering the cold?

He was not reckless. He took precautions, studied his props. But a life without risks was a life without desire. He had assumed his beloved bride and best friend had been up for the challenge. They had traversed the Alaskan tundra for their honeymoon, after all. Now, she shuddered from the cold, suffering annual bouts of bronchitis, as if it were its own season.

III.   Tall Tales
Goldilocks and the Three Bears was no joke! Her sixth-grade Language-Arts teacher, Ms. Reuter, had been right: fairy tales were woven from the real and the visceral, the everyday and the imagined. Gwendolyn's house was proof this early May: a mangled bird feeder and screen door pulled off the hinges one bright weekday morning as her mother baked banana bread in the kitchen.

Mrs. Dorchester had hollered when she heard the commotion before letting out a howl trailing clear down the valley at the Post Office. The Bear meant business as it thrashed its way through pots and pans hung high, knocked crockery crashing to the tile floor, until it frightened itself back out the doorway, but not before smashing the stained-glass chandelier swaying shakily in the aftermath of broken light— the commingling sounds of human and beast like the cacophonous cackles of crows on a high wire at dusk.

Clarissa shrieked with joy when she heard the tale, no thoughts
of the danger that lurked. She loved the wild kingdom. Let the bears reign,
lynxes lurch, eagles dive and soar. She couldn't ask for a lovelier place
to live. It was her heart's desire to work as a naturalist one day.
(Mrs. Dorchester had stated to the newspapers that the animal's intrusion
was both the most terrifying and exuberant experience of her life.
Clarissa understood this sentiment deeply, a fact she knew disturbed
her mother to the core.)

IV.   Earth Tones

In the end, it had come to this: broken sleep, soft winters, a
spring awakening in February, followed by deep freeze—and no food
to forage, whatsoever. Awake at last and feverish with hunger,
what was a beast to do? Aborted dreams, long-delayed feasts, the
promise of tender spring shoots and Jonquil bulbs the stuff of fairy tales
once rolling off the elders' tongues like ancient, torrid stream waters
glistening silver with fish fly-angling rocks. Famine is its own fuel. Even in
a summer of abundance, the memory of a first meal is its own seduction.
Mouths to feed, hides to thicken, the path to plenitude a muddle of instinct
and desire.

Firestorm: Checagou*
a protest poem

In the tall stalks of plenty where prairie meets plains
a city is born. Wild onions, wild fantasies.
Rivers run through it. Strident streams of Great-Lake currents
steady the flow of New-England merchant men:
princes and paupers, land pirates build the inestimable
sprawling of sweeping horizons.

Pelts fall to planks
warriors to mayors
dreams to currencies
forests to sweatshops.
Steam horses spar
with human life.
A river reversed
a pestilence delivered
downstream.

Necessity being the mother of invention,
steel structures rise, trains loop and dip
and the disassembly of beasts foretells
the Second Coming: lean iron horses feeding
scrap yards. Meanwhile,
the torpid transmigration of souls transpires:
dumped into Bubbly Creek later washed
down the mighty Mississippi, generations later
the river choking on silt.

*The Negro Speaks of Rivers.*** "I've seen fire and
I've seen rain."*** I've seen a lakefront open to parks
and people, wetlands overfed with fill. The vanishing
and the vanquished. Trains, planes, automobiles:
the confluence a gritty grid of asphalt angles and granite
canyons. Boats carrying the hopeful across the

*Native American term meaning skunk weed, smelly onion
** Langston Hughes, "The Negro Speaks of Rivers
***James Taylor, "Fire and Rain"

Great Dixie Divide. Mechanical men stacking flaxen
into elevators of wealth. Driven creators the brilliant
architects of modernity.

Flash forward to grim brick smokestack-like Habitats
for Humanity. Distinctive Projects. *Progress*. Native Sons
also rising. A Metamorphosis: onion fields to fertilizer beds
to killing parks slashed to the quick
with modern-day scythes and sickles;
drug-sick shepherds keeping watch on their flocks to part rival
weave from neighborhood chaff: flushing out futures like grouse
in the grasses, flesh falling from bone; sacrificial lambs, our heads
bowed to the heavens. *Our Country 'Tis of Thee.*
The ages echoing one into another,
aging with heartbreak, of thee I sing.

Rapid-fire consumption our
Gross Domestic Product.

Metal scrambles, screams through tissue;
just another Stormy Monday, the papers say. Strange Fruit falling
from the popular to arms. Farewell. Hand to hand combat. Friendly
fire. The gun runner wailing with the gospel choir.
"O, here's the shoe my baby wore, /But, baby, where are you?"****

A most uncivil war. Urban unrest. City of Big Shoulders, gangly adolescence.
Oh holy
night. Violence begets violence. O say,
can you see, by the dawn's dimming light.
The rocket's red glare the bombs bursting in air
gives proof through the night that our hearts are not there.
For the land of the free and the home of deep strife:
unsettled, unhealthy, unbidden. Rife
with sorrow.

****Dudley Randall, "The Ballad of Birmingham"

I speak of rivers
fire and rain.

Love's Loss

We met you just the once, an evening out:
Drinks first, a lavish meal; lights dimmed, mood lit.
No doubt joy reigned—charged atmosphere, bright bout.
Our daughter quick to place her hand on wrist
Of one whose moods traversed dark rivulets:
War raging in, deep pockets of great grief.
Ghosts haunt, terse words predict the mood forgets
Its mirth. No balm, no eucalyptus wreath
Crowns lovely youth of boundless hope, purged rage.
Though forge he does, the metallurgy of
Mind's eye: a thief of catastrophic wage
Steals heart to fight, heart laid to rest, deep love.
This mother's woe, though he is not her son,
Laments the age-old lie that war wins on.

In June
for Nia

Standing at the fence come evening—
dogs barking greetings,
dragonflies riding currents,
our grown children accomplished
and tucked into the world—
we exchange personal news,
take stock of political rumblings,
glacier melts, family updates,
the latest book and theater
temptations, neighbor gossip,
lake-water temperatures,
riptide alerts.

So many life and death events have skimmed
our shorelines: sailing tragedies, ailing mothers,
the fawn born in a wet heap on the
cold cement slab of your AC unit, your
husband still in awe; the rust-red fox meeting
my gaze, whitetails wading waters
Christmas day, cliff-size waves dredging up
timber from unknown depths.

You welcomed us—new neighbors—
to your Great-Lake paradise,
pioneer that you were.

The best of you, friend, is understated:
wry wit, hazel eyes darting amid
playful chortles, your friendship
steadfast as the summer solstice,
generous as its gift for the ages.

History Lessons

Chicago
in a remote marshland
thousands labored,
building empires
for the Barons
of fortune

Immigrants
sepia-toned tableaux:
silhouettes diffused in
smoke-lit tenements

Natural History
in a remote marshland
thousands migrate:
the forgotten Barons
of Majesty

Nancy L. Davis grew up in upstate New York, where the natural surroundings made an indelible impression on her language use and writing themes. After earning her MFA in Creative Writing & Literature from the University of Massachusetts in Amherst, she moved to Chicago, where she has lived since. Davis has published poetry, short fiction, book reviews and academic articles while also working first as a Writer/Producer of award-winning educational films and later as an Associate Professor of English. Her work has appeared in numerous journals, most recently, *Cutthroat, A Journal of the Arts, Philadelphia Stories, Route Nine, Primavera, The Ledge Magazine of Poetry & Fiction,* and *Cooweescoowee Journal of Arts & Letters*. Additionally, her work has garnered numerous awards, including First Place in the Sandy Crimmins National Poetry Prize, Finalist in the Joy Harjo Prize in Poetry, Second Place in The Ledge Short Fiction competition, Honorable Mention in the Lorian Hemingway Short Fiction Competition, and a poetry nomination for the Pushcart Prize. She lives with her husband, Richard Cappelletti, in Park Ridge, IL and Long Beach, IN, on Lake Michigan. Together, they have a daughter, Julia.